A New Era for Human Resources

Recruitment, Payroll, and Bonuses in the Age of Blockchain

Table of Contents

Chapter 1. Introduction

Welcome to an enlightening journey through a transformative era in Human Resources management! This Special Report, "A New Era for Human Resources: Recruitment, Payroll, and Bonuses in the Age of Blockchain", demystifies the intricacies of blockchain technology and its profound implications on HR practices. We delve into the exciting future where recruitment, payroll, and bonuses are streamlined, efficient, and reliable, anchored firmly on the bedrock of blockchain. Whether you're an HR expert searching for the most innovative practices, a tech enthusiast eager to decipher the business applications of blockchain, or just curious about the future of work, this comprehensive report is for you. Get ready to step into the future and embrace the revolution!

Chapter 2. Understanding Blockchain: A Primer for HR

Blockchain, typically associated with distributed ledger technology and cryptocurrencies like Bitcoin, is an innovation that has the potential to revolutionize several sectors, including Human Resources. In this chapter, we will explore the concepts underlying blockchain technology and how they can be adapted to transform HR practices. Refer to this chapter as your personal glossary and guide to understanding the revolutionary realm of blockchains in HR.

2.1. The Fundamentals of Blockchain

In simplest terms, blockchain is a decentralized database—instead of storing data on a single server, information on a blockchain is distributed across millions of computers globally. This data is stored in 'blocks' that are 'chained' together through cryptographic algorithms, hence the name 'Blockchain'.

Each block consists of a number of transactions. Once a block is filled with transactions, it is encrypted and linked to the previous block. This creates a chain of blocks, or a blockchain. What makes this structure unique is that once a block is added to the chain, its data cannot be changed. This immutability imbues the entire system with a high level of security and transparency.

One key feature of blockchain is its decentralization. There's no central authority controlling the data or transactions— instead, they are verified by the network participants. This eliminates the need for intermediaries, reduces cost, and increases efficiency.

Another feature is transparency. All members of the blockchain network have access to the entire chain, although personal identities are hidden behind cryptographic pseudonyms. This allows an unparalleled level of public verification and auditability.

2.2. Blockchain in HR: A Preview

Though it seems daunting, understanding blockchain's potential applications in HR is the first step to unlocking its benefits. In simpler terms, think of blockchain as a vast, globally accessible spreadsheet that can be viewed but not changed. Any HR-related documentation, certifications, or data could be safely stored, verified, and shared with this technology, minimizing paperwork and eliminating potential errors.

2.3. Encryption and Cryptographic Hashes

Each transaction in a block is encrypted using a cryptographic hash function. This function transforms the input information into a unique string of characters, which is nearly impossible to decode. This helps ensure the confidentiality and security of data.

The security of blockchain comes from its structure. Once a block is formed and linked to the chain, altering any information within it would require changing the information in all subsequent blocks, which is computationally impractical. Thus, any data once added on a blockchain network remains uncorrupted and immutable.

2.4. Smart Contracts

Blockchain enables the use of 'Smart Contracts', which are self-executing contracts with the terms directly written into code. They automatically execute actions when predefined conditions are met. Examples of potential smart contract applications in HR could include automatically releasing payments when a work deliverable is completed or automatically onboard a new hire once all necessary conditions are met.

2.5. Decentralized Autonomous Organization (DAO)

A DAO is an organization represented by rules encoded as a computer program that is transparent, controlled by organizational members and not influenced by a central government. DAOs can allow whole organizations to run with superhuman transparency and efficiency, nature of which is best leveraged by HR.

In the next chapters, we delve into specifics, exploring how these elements of blockchain technology can revolutionize HR processes like recruitment, payroll, and bonuses. Throughout the rest of this report, we will continue to refer back to these fundamental concepts. So, this primer on blockchain is an essential reference point, offering a strong foundation for understanding the rest of the transformation that lies ahead.

Blockchain is not just a technological shift. It is a rethink of the fundamental infrastructures that underpin our HR systems. As we explore each of these potential applications further, embrace this new era of change and the seemingly limitless possibilities it offers for Human Resources. Welcome to the future, where blockchain meets, matches, and magnifies the true potential of HR!

Chapter 3. The Intersection of Blockchain and Human Resources

The advent of blockchain technology marks a milestone in the digital realm that is transforming a multitude of industries. Its disruptive power is now seeping into areas untapped before, particularly Human Resources (HR). Let's embark on an exploration into the overlap of blockchain technology and HR, investigating how it's reshaping traditional practices.

3.1. Blockchain – a brief primer

Before pinpointing the intersections of blockchain and HR, it's worth familiarizing ourselves with blockchain technology itself. Outlining its clear, concise description, blockchain is a decentralized, distributable digital ledger, recording transactions across multiple devices, so that every involved block of the chain can validate them. The unique cryptographic principle imbibes security, transparency, and immutability, making it nearly impossible to tamper with the data once recorded.

3.2. Transforming Recruitment

One of the HR sectors impacted significantly by blockchain is recruitment and employee onboarding. HR professionals spend considerable time and effort verifying prospective employees' credentials, including academic achievements, professional experiences, and other qualifications.

Blockchain can effectively streamline this process. Individuals could have their professional records stored on a blockchain, which would be verified by a trusted party and hence, not need multiple re-verifications. This system ensures only verified data enters the blockchain, eliminating the possibility of fraudulent claims and counterfeit documents.

3.3. Enhancing Payroll Process

Blockchain can revolutionalize cross-border payroll and benefits distribution. Traditional international payments often involve multiple intermediaries, leading to high transaction costs, possible human errors, and longer processing time.

Enter blockchain – its peer-to-peer, decentralized nature enables direct, quicker, and less costly transactions. Furthermore, it eliminates the potential error-introducing intermediaries. Using blockchain-based cryptocurrencies (like Bitcoin) for payroll can be especially beneficial for remote international workers, as it ensures accurate payment without foreign exchange fees or regulatory hurdles.

3.4. Secure Data Storage

HR departments handle vast troves of confidential employee data, making secure storage a priority. Traditional centralized data systems are prone to single point failures and cyberattacks, risking data breaches.

Blockchain can enhance security with its distributed, encrypted safeguards. Each block containing data is encrypted uniquely – to alter one block; a cybercriminal would need to modify all the preceding blocks in the chain across all copies in the network. This degree of complexity makes blockchain one of the best tools to protect HR data.

3.5. Immutability and Compliance

Regulatory compliance and audit trails have been pain points for HR, owing to the necessity for transparency and traceability in procedures such as payroll and benefits distribution.

Immutability is one of blockchain's core characteristics, meaning once data is added, it's nearly impossible to change it. This attribute combined with blockchain's chronological transaction order makes it an ideal tool for maintaining accurate, tamper-proof records that can demonstrate compliance and simplify audit trails.

3.6. Rethinking performance bonuses and rewards

Employers are innovating incentive systems through blockchain. Companies can issue blockchain-based tokens as part of the incentive or reward programs. Employees can then convert these tokens into different forms of currency, or use them for various services offered by the company or its partners.

This approach not only introduces a novel way of handling bonuses but also encourages a sense of ownership and active engagement in the corporate ecosystem.

3.7. Conclusion

In summary, the intersection of blockchain and HR heralds a future where advanced technology enhances efficiency, transparency, and reliability in HR practices. Although it's still nascent in its application and acceptance, potential benefits of blockchain in HR cannot be underplayed. As the world of work evolves, adopting innovative technologies such as blockchain becomes paramount not merely to stay relevant but to lead in a rapidly transforming landscape.

There will be challenges and practical considerations when deploying these technologies. Issues such as integration with existing systems, regulatory acceptance, and public trust in blockchain's potential will need addressing. Nevertheless, pioneering organizations are already on the path of adopting blockchain in HR processes, and it's only a matter of time before it becomes mainstream. These developments make it more important than ever for HR professionals to understand this evolving technology and its implications. Through knowledge and understanding, they can be equipped to harness the significant opportunities that this new era presents.

Chapter 4. Recruitment Reinvented: Blockchain's Implications

Traditional recruitment processes are notoriously slow, inefficient, and susceptible to human error and bias. Coupled with increasing competition for top talent, navigating these waters can be an excruciating task. However, blockchain technology has arrived as a potential game-changer, promising a future where recruitment methods are not only efficient and reliable, but also transparent and equitable.

4.1. Understanding the Blockchain

Blockchain is a decentralized and distributed digital ledger. It uniformly stores information across multiple systems, reducing the chance of it being manipulated from a single source. Each piece of data in a blockchain is stored in a 'block,' and each block is linked to the previous and the subsequent block in a 'chain.' This gives blockchain its name and ensures transparency and security since all changes made in a block need to be approved by the majority and the entire chain is affected by the alteration.

4.2. Blockchain & Candidate Verification

One of the most frustrating parts of recruitment for both HR managers and job seekers is the verification of credentials. Checking certifications, references, and job histories can often take weeks, not to mention the hassles involved if an applicant has worked internationally. A significant portion of HR's time, resources, and budget is dedicated to these processes.

But with blockchain, the process can be radically streamlined. Once an institution, such as a university or a previous employer, verifies a credential or piece of information about a candidate and enters it into a blockchain, it stays verified forever. The information cannot be altered without the consensus of all parties involved, ensuring authenticity and eliminating the need for excessive verification in successive recruitments.

4.3. Global Recruitment & Blockchain

Global recruitment is another area that stands to benefit greatly from blockchain technology. The globalization of business requires a diverse talent pool, often necessitating the hiring of international employees—a process frequently delayed by cross-border legal and verification hassles.

Blockchain removes the boundaries of geographical limitations and allows for a smoother international recruitment process. The verified data within the blockchain can be accessed anytime, by any employer, irrespective of the geographical location. This instantaneous, secure verification of credentials can significantly expedite the process of global hiring, reducing the wait time and administrative costs.

4.4. Eliminating Bias with Blockchain

Unconscious bias, a prejudice that we aren't aware we harbor, remains a significant challenge in recruitment. No matter how meticulously HR professionals try to eliminate these biases, some still creep into the process. Using blockchain technology can help reduce this concern to a considerable extent.

By utilizing a smart contract, recruiters can program immutable 'if-then' conditions into the hiring algorithm. For example, 'if' a candidate has more than five years' experience and a Master's degree, 'then' shortlist for an interview. As blockchain ensures that the algorithm's functioning is transparent and unaltered, reliance on such technology reduces the scope for unconscious bias.

4.5. The Use of Tokens in Recruitment

In terms of incentivizing, blockchain can also utilize tokens, which are digital assets within a blockchain. These tokens can be used to incentivize people to action. For instance, companies could incentivize potential candidates or existing employees with tokens for referring potential hires.

4.6. The Future of Recruitment

While the practical implementation of blockchain in recruitment is still in its nascent stages, the potential good it can bring is substantial. Blockchain holds the promise of a more secure, transparent, and fast-paced recruiting process that is advantageous for both employers and candidates.

It paves the way for reducing administrative costs, hastening the recruitment process, facilitating global hiring, and eliminating bias from the hiring process. The era of blockchain in HR opens a realm of enormous possibilities—where blockchain is institutionalized and every credential exists verified and immaculate, ready for instantaneous access and assessment.

Companies, recruiters, and HR professionals must ready themselves to embrace this paradigm shift toward blockchain technology. It's not just about staying ahead in the race for talent—it's about transforming the very face of recruitment. With blockchain, the future of recruitment isn't just promising; it's already taking shape.

In conclusion, blockchain is more than just a revolutionary technology—it is a shift towards transparency, security, and efficiency. The blockchain in HR recruitment will not only streamline and optimize the process but also provide an unbiased, transparent, and secure mechanism. And with the added benefit of saving time and money, the transformation is set to revolutionize the industry.

Chapter 5. Payroll in the Blockchain Era: Transparency and Security

The advent of blockchain technology introduces an innovative dimension to traditional HR operations and promises to revamp many areas, one of which is payroll.

Payroll management has always been a fundamental business operation, ensuring that employees are compensated promptly and accurately. However, it remains plagued by inefficiencies and errors stemming largely from its intricacy, especially in scenarios involving multi-country or international businesses. Fortunately, blockchain technology provides a potential remedy to these challenges.

5.1. Payroll Transparency: From Illusion to Reality

In traditional payroll systems, transparency is an aspired ideal that's seldom achieved. It's often challenging to manage and audit payments, tax deductions, benefits, and added complexities like currency exchange rates in international transactions.

Blockchain, a decentralized and distributed ledger, promises transparency because every transaction within the network is recorded transparently and cannot be altered. This transparency is particularly valuable in payroll management.

By integrating the payroll system with blockchain, companies can create an immutable and transparent record for every monetary transaction. This means that employees can personally verify their compensation, benefits, deductions and paid taxes, fostering confidence and trust in the system.

5.2. Security: The Blockchain Defense

While the criticality of data security in payroll management is recognized throughout all industries, it remains a significant challenge. Traditional centralized databases are susceptible to attacks that could potentially lead to the loss or theft of critical employee data.

This is where blockchain's inherent security properties come into play. The data on a blockchain are stored across a network of computers, making a single point of failure impossible. In addition, the implementation of cryptographic functions furthers the security of information. Therefore, blockchain could significantly bolster the security of payroll data.

5.3. Decentralization: The operational edge

The decentralized nature of blockchain brings a unique operational advantage. In a traditional system, employing a workforce across borders entails managing multiple payment systems, conforming to a variety of local labor laws, handling fluctuating exchange rates, and more.

With blockchain, the payroll process is streamlined and simplified. As a global ledger, blockchain allows businesses to consolidate all their operations into one system, irrespective of geographical boundaries. The implications of this are far-reaching; companies can execute cross-border payments swiftly and efficiently, without the need for intermediaries. This significantly reduces costs and enhances the speed, thus improving the overall payroll management process.

5.4. Smart Contracts: Automation and Accuracy

Smart contracts represent another exciting aspect of blockchain technology. They are programmed contracts which self-execute when certain pre-set conditions are met. In the context of payroll, it offers automation and higher accuracy.

Companies can program smart contracts for salary payments, and the remunerations would be automatically transferred to an employee once the pre-set conditions (usually the completion of a task or a particular time) are met. Blockchain's immutable nature ensures that the smart contracts cannot be altered or deleted once initiated. This infuses accuracy, speed, and trust into the payroll system.

5.5. The Future of Payroll with Blockchain

While blockchain provides a fascinating solution to many longstanding payroll problems, it's worth noting there are hurdles to clear before fully realizing its potential. From technical complexity to regulatory concerns, these obstacles need to be tackled before wholesale adoption can occur.

Yet, the future points towards increased convergence between blockchain and HR processes. The transparency, security, operational benefits, and efficiency it brings can revolutionize payroll management in ways we can only just begin to imagine.

It is an exciting time for HR professionals and businesses alike. Some companies have already started piloting blockchain for their HR practices, primarily focusing on payroll. These preliminary experiments serve as stepping stones to a future where HR processes are streamlined, efficient, and transparent, echoing blockchain's core tenets.

In conclusion, the convergence of blockchain and payroll management holds significant promise and potential. As HR professionals, business leaders, and regulator's understanding and acceptance of this technology continue to grow, we might be looking at the dawn of a new era in HR management. The blockchain era!

Chapter 6. Revolutionising Bonuses with Blockchain: A Rewarding Change

Bonuses have always been an influential component in boosting employee morale, providing motivation, and triggering impressive performance. Yet, the rewarding system has its fair share of complexity, especially in adhering to the rules of transparency and clarity. The journey of implementing bonus schemes, the quantification of bonus amounts, and the ultimate transfer to the respective employee's accounts can, at times, be convoluted. Blockchain technology presents a promising opportunity to transform and simplify this age-old method of remuneration. By introducing an efficient, fast, transparent, and secure system, blockchain has immense potential to revolutionize the bonus system.

6.1. Shaping Transparency with Blockchain-Driven Bonuses

Transparency is the cornerstone of effective communication and trust between an organization and its employees. However, traditional bonus systems may lack this essential characteristic, fostering discontent and miscommunication. Bonus calculations can be complex, with varying factors such as performance metrics, job role, and more contributing towards the final figure. This complexity breeds ambiguity and dissatisfactions, but blockchain has the potential to alleviate these concerns.

Blockchain, considered a 'decentralized ledger', can record transactions across several computers in such a way that the registered transactions cannot be altered retroactively. This characteristic implies that once an employee's bonus determination criteria and amount are uploaded on the blockchain, they cannot be changed unilaterally. It ensures a seamless audit trail and complete transparency. Given this feature, employees would trust their organizations more, as they would know the precise reasons that affected their bonuses and by how much.

6.2. Minimizing Errors in Bonus Processing with Blockchain

Despite the advancements in technology, manual processes still govern several HR operations, including bonus processing. These manual operations often open the door to human error, causing inconsistencies and engendering employee dissatisfaction. This problem could become a thing of the past with blockchain, which empowers the bonus calculation process with automation.

Smart contracts, which are self-executing contracts with the terms of the agreement directly written into code, ensure automation and reduce errors. Smart contracts driven bonus systems would calculate bonus amounts by predetermined rules and execute the payment without manual intervention. These contracts can also guarantee that the bonuses are paid on time. The implementation of a smart contract system in bonus processing would mean fewer calculation errors and hence, fewer disputes.

6.3. Ensuring Equity in Bonus Payment through Blockchain

Equity in bonus payments is an essential component of employee satisfaction. With traditional methods, there may be unfortunate instances of favouritism or mistakes in distribution. Utilizing blockchain can significantly mitigate these issues, introducing a level of fairness.

By recording all performance metrics and bonus calculations on the blockchain, it will ensure that bonus payments are equitable and determined solely by the employee's performance or other quantifiable metrics stated in the smart contract. This fairness can offer a significant boost to employee morale and productivity as employees recognize that their efforts are valued based on merit, not favouritism or error.

6.4. Streamlining International Bonus Payments with Blockchain

For multinational corporations, distributing bonuses across different locations often involves dealing with multiple currencies, foreign exchange rates, and international banking. These complexities pose challenges such as increased costs, longer processing times, and potential discrepancies.

Distributed ledger technology can streamline these processes significantly, making bonus distribution less cumbersome and more efficient. By employing cryptocurrency for bonus distribution, blockchain could eliminate the need for currency conversion and reduce transaction times, thus bringing down costs and accelerating the bonus payment process.

Chapter 7. Embrace the Change, Empower the Employees

It is safe to say that we are standing at the precipice of a new era in human resources management. The implications of blockchain technology go well beyond bonus management: offering secure, transparent, and efficient solutions capable of revolutionizing HR processes.

Blockchain's unique attributes of transparency, security, and efficiency position it well for the task of reinventing bonus distribution. Its potential to reduce disputes and foster trust can empower organizations to build stronger relationships with their employees. Moreover, blockchain eliminates geographical barriers, giving companies the power to reward their employees promptly and fairly, irrespective of their location.

It's time to move away from legacy systems and archaic practices. The advent of blockchain heralds a progressive and resilient future for bonus distribution. Embracing blockchain is not only a step towards efficient management but could also signify an anticipated and commendable stride towards a rewarding and transparent workplace.

Chapter 8. Case Studies: Successful Blockchain Implementation in HR

The advent of blockchain technology has been a game changer in numerous industries, carving new pathways for innovation, efficiency, and reliability in managing complex business processes. The Human Resources (HR) domain, tasked with the crucial responsibility of managing people – the most valuable asset of any organization – is no exception. Numerous case studies provide a glimpse into how blockchain has successfully been implemented into HR functions and its transformative potential.

8.1. Blockchain in Recruitment

The recruitment process has always been resource-intensive, requiring checks for candidate's identity, qualifications, experience and skills. Even with digital advancements, the process can be prone to inaccuracies and frauds. But organizations are now looking to blockchain to address some of these challenges.

Corporate giants like Infosys have placed their bets on blockchain's potential to reform the recruitment process. In 2019, the firm launched a blockchain-based employee validation platform called 'Infosys Information Grid.' This application serves as an immutable, verifiable ledger of employee data, such as qualifications and work experience, which is authenticated by the issuing institutions and former employers.

Not only has this boosted efficiency by reducing the time taken for validation checks, but it has also significantly reduced fraud. Infosys Information Grid is a prime example of how blockchain can bring trust, ease, and accuracy to the recruitment process.

8.2. Blockchain for Payroll Management

Payroll management, especially for multinational organizations, can be a daunting task, grappling with factors such as volatile foreign exchange rates, different tax regulations, and transaction times. Typically, organizations resort to third-party financial institutions, which adds to the expense and time taken for cross-border funds transfer.

GMO Internet Group, a Japanese internet company, addressed this complex challenge by adopting Bitcoin for remunerating its international workforce. Since 2018, their employees have had the option to receive a portion of their salary in Bitcoin, minimizing the need for currency conversion and reducing transaction times.

Implementing blockchain into payroll has not only simplified processes for the organization but also added a layer of security. Every transaction made on the blockchain can be tracked, enhancing accountability and making fraud detection easier.

8.3. Implementing Smart Contracts for Bonuses

Incentive and bonus pay-outs can be a complex task, given the need for clear performance assessment, accurate calculations, and tracking of payouts. Blockchain can address these challenges through smart contracts – self-executing contracts with the terms of agreement directly written into code.

AXA, one of the world's leading insurance firms, has pioneered the use of blockchain for managing bonuses through their product, "Fizzy". The unique insurance product, operational since 2017, automatically compensates customers if their flights are delayed by over two hours.

In such a model, HR departments can create smart contracts for their employees that define the terms for bonuses or incentives. Once the predefined conditions are met - like reaching a sales target or completing a project within the deadline - the bonus is automatically dispatched. This eliminates the need for manual tracking and calculation, reducing errors and disputes.

8.4. Conclusion

Investigating real-world applications of blockchain implementation in HR suggests a promising and virtually limitless future. The cases of Infosys, GMO Internet Group, and AXA demonstrate the immense potential of integrating blockchain into HR functions - from simplified recruitment and efficient payroll management to error-free bonus payouts.

While blockchain adoption still faces challenges like standardization and regulatory concerns, the benefits – such as transparency, security, and efficiency – cannot be overlooked. As businesses increasingly recognize the value of blockchain technology, the adoption curve is likely to accelerate, heralding a new future for human resources management.

Expect more HR functions to follow suit, using blockchain technology to transform their operations and strategies in the years to come. The organizations that manage to effectively harness the power of this emerging technology will undoubtedly stand at the forefront of innovation, setting new benchmarks in human resources management.

The revolution has just begun, and blockchain is at the helm, steering the world of HR into an exciting, unprecedented future.

In the next section, we will explore the challenges and potential solutions in adopting blockchain in HR management, providing valuable insights to those looking to take the plunge into this transformative technology. Keep reading to equip yourself with the knowledge that could be the difference between successful and unsuccessful blockchain adoption. The future of HR is here, and it's called blockchain.

Chapter 9. Challenges and Concerns: Navigating Blockchain in HR

As organizations worldwide endeavor to juggle with the prospects and challenges birthed from the blockchain revolution, several key issues take the foreground. Each poses its unique conundrum and warrants serious considerations and action to exploit the full benefits of blockchain in Human Resources (HR) management.

9.1. Blockchain's Complexity and Technicality

Blockchain was originally designed to enable Bitcoin transactions, and the technology was never meant to be simple. It involves cryptographic principles, distributed systems, peer-to-peer networks, and consensus algorithms, among other complicated constructs not easily understandable for the average HR personnel.

In a field where the majority of professionals come from a non-technical background, the blockchain's complexity can be quite daunting, leading to potential resistance to its adoption. However, this challenge may be addressed through proper training and awareness sessions, making it crucial for organizations to invest in capacity-building initiatives. Additionally, organizations can foster partnerships with external blockchain experts or consultants to break down the complexities and enhance HR professionals' understanding.

9.2. Technical Infrastructure Assessment and Upgrade

Successfully integrating blockchain into HR operations necessitates a comprehensive and rigorous evaluation of an organization's existing technical infrastructure. This includes reviewing data storage capacities, servers, networking architecture, and cyber-security processes, among others. Given its decentralized nature, blockchain requires robust systems and high storage capacities.

Any gaps identified in this evaluation should be addressed, possibly requiring significant financial investments. IT infrastructure acceptable to current HR systems may not be sufficient or compatible with blockchain technology. It is thus critical that leadership recognizes the need for any significant infrastructure overhauls as inevitable investments for creating a more efficient, transparent, and reliable HR function.

9.3. Data Privacy and Protection

One of the most pressing concerns stemming from the widespread use of blockchain in HR is data privacy and protection. Blockchain's decentralized, immutable nature can be a double-edged sword when it comes to data management. Once data is added to the network, it is practically impossible to modify or delete it, posing potential risks to users' privacy.

Organizations must take care to consider how they handle sensitive data, such as employee records and personal identifying information, and ensure it cannot be exploited. GDPR and other privacy regulations emphasise on the 'right to be forgotten', which seems inherently incongruous with the immutable nature of blockchain. Framing policies around these regulatory nuances will be essential for HR departments.

9.4. Regulatory Landscape

The rapidly evolving nature of blockchain technology often surpasses regulatory frameworks, creating a 'wild west' scenario where legislation is often playing catch-up. From a corporate standpoint, ramifications related to data protection standards, taxation policies, contractual obligations, transborder data flow, could all be deeply influenced due to blockchain's distributed, borderless nature.

HR departments must partner with their legal teams to ensure all blockchain-related applications comply with existing and potential future legislation. Regulatory vigilance would be key to navigating this realm of legislative ambiguity.

9.5. Change Management

As with any future-proofing initiative, harnessing the potential of blockchain in HR involves a dramatic cultural shift within the organization. HR personnel would need to be comfortable with transitioning to a more transparent, decentralized mode of operation.

Effective communication of the perceived benefits of blockchain adoption, addressing potential concerns, and assurances of continuous learning support could be instrumental in managing this change. Such change management initiatives demand thoughtful planning and execution, given the diverse array of stakeholders involved - from HR staff to employees across the entire organization.

9.6. Cost of Implementation and ROI Analysis

Deploying blockchain within HR operations is likely to be a cost-intensive affair. Coupled with an ambiguous return on investment

(ROI), this poses yet another challenge for HR leaders stressing budgetary concerns. They need to weigh the initial setup costs, ongoing costs in terms of upgrades and maintenance, and potential savings through efficiency gains and reduction in HR fraud.

Conducting a thorough cost-benefit analysis before rolling out blockchain applications can help organizations rationalize the financial viability and understand the potential payback period.

The blockchain revolution in HR remains in its early stages, and while its promise is tantalizing, a cautious, careful navigation through these challenges is the only way forward. Ensuring an understanding of the technology, vigilance towards the regulatory environment, robust change management, and thorough analysis of cost and infrastructure considerations, will all play a crucial role in making the journey a resounding success.

Chapter 10. Navigating Legal and Ethical Considerations in Blockchain HR

To successfully implement blockchain technology in HR operations, organizations must navigate a maze of legal and ethical considerations. This encompasses everything from ensuring concerns surrounding data privacy are adequately addressed, to ensuring adherence to laws regulating employee compensation and benefits.

10.1. Understanding the Complexities of Data Privacy

Data privacy is a pressing concern when implementing blockchain in HR. Unlike conventional databases, blockchain transactions are inherently immutable and transparent. This poses unique challenges for HR departments that handle sensitive employee data, including payroll details, benefits information, personal identifiers, performance metrics, and more.

When designing HR systems based on blockchain technology, organizations must balance the need for transparency with their legal obligations to protect sensitive personal data. Factors to consider include - where data will be stored, who will have access to it, how it will be protected, and how long it will be retained for.

Organizations should map out data flows, identifying where blockchain can be used to improve efficiency and security, and where traditional systems may be better suited. Special attention should be paid to any processes involving sensitive personal data, with measures put in place to ensure strict compliance with data protection laws.

10.2. Regulatory Compliance in Employee Compensation and Benefits

Blockchain can be used to automate payroll and benefits distribution, speeding up processes and improving accuracy. However, organizations must ensure that these automated systems comply with labor laws, wage and hour laws, and other relevant regulations.

In the US, for example, the Fair Labor Standards Act (FLSA) sets minimum wage rates, overtime rules, and other wage-related regulations. Companies must design their blockchain-based payroll systems to adhere to these rules, and regularly review and update them in line with any regulatory changes.

A similar approach should be taken to benefits distribution. For example, blockchain could be used to create a transparent and efficient system for awarding and tracking employee stock options. However, such a system must comply with regulations governing securities and employee benefits, such as those set out in the Employee Retirement Income Security Act (ERISA). Companies should consult with legal and financial advisors to ensure compliance.

10.3. Managing Legal Risks Associated with Smart Contracts

The use of smart contracts is a key aspect of blockchain HR. These self-executing contracts with the terms of the agreement directly written into lines of code can streamline many HR processes, from recruitment to payroll. However, they also present unique legal challenges.

Organizations need to ensure their smart contracts comply with contract laws in the jurisdictions they operate in to avoid legal disputes. The immutability of blockchain-based smart contracts can be both a blessing and a curse – once a contract is set in motion, it cannot be easily altered or canceled, so any mistakes or oversights can have serious ramifications.

Additionally, the legal status of smart contracts may vary between jurisdictions. While some countries may recognize them as legally binding contracts, others may not. Companies operating across multiple jurisdictions should seek legal advice to ensure their smart contracts are enforceable worldwide.

10.4. Ethical Considerations in Applying Blockchain for HR

While blockchain can enhance privacy, security, and efficiency in HR, it also introduces new ethical considerations. Organizations must ensure their use of blockchain aligns with their corporate ethics guidelines and societal norms of fairness, privacy, and transparency.

Additionally, blockchain can disrupt power dynamics within organizations. Its decentralized nature eliminates the need for intermediaries and can reduce the influence of powerful individuals or departments. While this can increase efficiency and reduce biases, it may also lead to resistance from those affected. Organizations must manage these changes carefully to avoid conflicts.

The ethical implications of transparency within blockchain should also be carefully considered. While increased transparency can lead to better accountability, it can also risk infringing on employees' privacy rights if not handled properly.

Organizations need to strike a balance between transparency, security, and privacy - the full potential of blockchain in HR can only be realized when all three are harmoniously intertwined.

Organizations embarking on the blockchain journey must consider these legal and ethical aspects carefully, and plan accordingly. Through a blend of caution, innovation, and adherence to legal and ethical principles, organizations can harness the power of blockchain to transform their HR operations while assuring a safe, secure, and responsible transition.

Chapter 11. Future Outlook: Evolving HR in the Age of Blockchain

In the past decade, blockchain, a transparent, decentralized database system, has surged in popularity and adoption due to its promise of offering unprecedented security and promoting trustless interactions. As the technology continues to penetrate different sectors, the field of Human Resource Management (HRM) is not being left behind. Given the decentralized and transparent nature of blockchain, it points towards an evolution of HRM processes that are not only efficient but also secure, robust, and reliable.

11.1. Recruitment Process Revolutionized by Blockchain

A key process in HRM is the recruitment of new employees. Traditional recruitment processes, often characterized by extensive manual verification of applicant credentials and negotiation of employment contracts, can be laborious, error-prone, and susceptible to fraud.

Blockchain technology could redefine this process, making it faster, easier, and safer. For instance, blockchain-based platforms could store verified educational qualifications and professional experience of potential employees, accessible to employers by permission. This erases the need to manually verify qualifications and reduces the hiring time significantly.

Further, the negotiation of contracts and agreements could be efficiently expedited through blockchain-based smart contracts. These self-executing contracts with the terms of the agreement directly written into code automate traditionally tedious processes, thus driving operational efficiency.

11.2. Payroll Simplification and Security

Payroll management forms another vital function of HR, often posing numerous challenges, especially for businesses operating globally. Dealing with different tax regulations, fluctuating currencies, and different payment schedules can make payroll management a nightmare.

Blockchain could streamline these processes while enhancing security and accuracy. As a distributed ledger, blockchain can simplify the calculation and deduction of appropriate taxes from employee salaries, convert them into the required currency and disburse payments on predefined dates.

This not only eliminates the need for intermediaries and reduces processing times, but also ensures that employees receive precisely the right amount at the right time. Furthermore, due to the immutable nature of blockchain records, fraudulent activities can be substantially minimized.

11.3. Incentives and Bonuses

Employee reward systems are crucial for motivation and retention. However, the distribution of bonuses and incentives often falls prey to unfair practices, delays, and disputes.

The transparent, immutable, and decentralized nature of blockchain can solve these issues. Blockchain, in conjunction with smart contracts, can be used to enforce incentive structures and disperse bonuses when predefined criteria are met.

Such a system would not only ensure fair incentive allocation, but also foster trust among employees and boost morale. It could also eliminate unnecessary disputes regarding rewards, as all transactions would be time-stamped and recorded on the blockchain.

11.4. Challenges in Implementing Blockchain in HR

While the potential of blockchain technology in revamping HR is vast, the path to implementation isn't free from challenges. Technological complexity, lack of legal and regulatory clarity, and adoption resistance are some of the potential hurdles.

It is imperative for organizations to partner with blockchain experts or consultancies, who can guide the organization through the implementation. Simultaneously, companies should work closely with legal teams to ensure compliance with local regulations and international standards.

11.5. Concluding Thoughts

The unprecedented potential of blockchain technology to transform our world has become impossible to ignore. In the HRM field, blockchain promises to overhaul traditional practices, introducing a new era of efficiency, security, and transparency.

The integration of blockchain into HR processes can revolutionize recruitment, payroll management, and reward systems. However, comprehensive research, meticulous planning, and collaboration with tech and legal experts is essential before embarking on this transformative journey.

Technologies like blockchain continue to blur the lines between disciplines. Hence, HR professionals of the future need to equip themselves with a wide array of skills, not limited to their traditional domain. Embracing this evolution will unquestionably yield a future where HRM truly becomes a strategic partner in organizational success.

Overall, the future outlook on the evolving HR in the age of blockchain appears promising. As we navigate through this exciting era, this technology promises to further reaffirm its game-changing potential in the HR landscape, marking a new chapter in human resource management.

Chapter 12. Roadmap to Adoption: Implementing Blockchain in Your HR Department

The era of blockchain in Human Resources management is here, and it brings implications for data security, transparency, and operational efficiency. It is crucial for HR professionals to understand the potential applications and benefits of this technology, as well as the steps required for its implementation.

12.1. Understanding Blockchain

Before proceeding with the implementation of blockchain, it's essential to comprehend what it fundamentally is and how it works. At its core, blockchain consists of a chain of blocks — each block representing a transaction or a set of transactions. Each transaction is assigned a unique cryptographic signature, ensuring the immutability and traceability of each transaction. Trust in a blockchain network depends on its collective effort, meaning all parties involved in a transaction play a role in validating it.

For businesses, an understanding of blockchain should focus on its three guiding principles: decentralization, transparency, and security.

12.2. Decentralization and Why It Matters

In a blockchain network, any operation or transaction isn't controlled by a single central authority, rather it's verified and validated by multiple nodes (participants) in the network. This aspect brings democratisation into data management, diminishing the chances of fraud and reducing the reliance on a single party for maintaining and verifying data.

With HR departments often handling tremendous volumes of sensitive employee data, decentralization could spell the end of massive data beaches by eliminating single points of failure in data storage and management.

12.3. Transparency: Key to Building Trust

One significant benefit of implementing blockchain in an HR department is the boost in transparency. The blockchain ledger records every transaction in a transparent and traceable manner. Any changes to the data are recorded immediately and the record is visible to all participants.

This contributes to trust-building as all stakeholders have an equal view of transactions. For HR, this could mean an end to numerous disputes related to payments, benefits, and other transactions, thereby promoting a healthy workplace environment.

12.4. The Security Promise

A unique feature of blockchain is the immutability of its transactions. Once a block is added to the chain, it cannot be altered or deleted. Additionally, transactions cannot be added without the consensus of the network participants, adding another layer of data security.

Implementing this level of security can help HR departments reduce risks associated with data breaches, identity theft, and fraud, significantly enhancing the integrity of HR practices.

12.5. Steps to Implement Blockchain in HR

After grasping the fundamentals, principles, and benefits of blockchain, the next crucial step involves understanding how to implement it in your HR department.

12.5.1. Evaluate the Need

The first step of any major technology implementation is the assessment of need. Understand where its application could provide the most compelling benefits. Do you need blockchain for secure payroll management? Or maybe you are seeking an efficient way to verify candidate qualifications during the recruitment process. Evaluating your need is the foundation on which you build your blockchain strategy.

12.5.2. Select the Right Blockchain Platform

While blockchain is the underlying technology, numerous blockchain platforms provide different features. Some enterprises might require a platform with smart contract functionality, while others might prioritize transaction speed or security. Align the blockchain platform choice with your identified needs.

12.5.3. Assemble a Skilled Team

Having a dedicated team is vital for the successful implementation of any technology. You may need blockchain experts, software developers, and possibly legal consultants on your team. However, the heart and soul of this team should be someone who understands both HR processes and the technology.

12.5.4. Pilot a Project

Before a full-scale implementation, it would be wise to conduct a pilot project. This could help identify potential problems and allow for design tweaks before committing massive resources. It also provides an opportunity for your team to adapt to the new technology and acquire vital hands-on experience.

12.5.5. Integrate with Existing Systems

Design your blockchain implementation to integrate seamlessly with existing HR systems. This will minimize disruption to ongoing operations and generate buy-in from users who might be resistant to change.

12.6. Standards and Compliance

While implementing a disruptive technology like blockchain, adhering to regional policies, industry-specific norms, and organizational standards is paramount. Engaging legal guidance throughout the implementation process is highly recommended to ensure compliance with all regulations.

12.7. Training and Support

It's crucial to remember that successful technology implementation does not solely rely on technical teams. It also requires training for end-users, HR teams, and management. Providing solid support and training would ensure that everyone involved understands and can utilize the new system effectively.

The HR landscape is changing rapidly. It's time to adapt and innovate, embracing blockchain and the opportunities it brings to the HR field. Implementing blockchain in HR management can unlock unimaginable efficiencies, but it isn't without its challenges. By understanding, planning, implementing the right way, and ensuring strong support, the road towards a new HR era is much smoother and well within reach.

41

www.ingramcontent.com/pod-product-compliance
Lightning Source LLC
Chambersburg PA
CBHW071011260726
48661CB00007B/2907